WHAT IF JESUS WERE
A NEW YORK CITY
FIREFIGHTER?

WHAT IF JESUS WERE A NEW YORK CITY FIREFIGHTER?

A STORY BORN ON SEPTEMBER 11, 2001

Martin E. Coleman
and Thomas J. Vito

VICO
Publishing Inc.

Hauppauge
New York

VICO Publishing, Inc.
1112 Devonshire Road
Hauppauge, New York 11788
www.vicopublishing.com
www.whatifjesuswere.com

ISBN: 978-0-9850541-0-6

This book is available for bulk purchases at
special discounts for promotional and premium use.
The Publisher can create special printings and excerpts,
personalized and tailored to meet the special needs
of institutions, associations, the corporate
and business community.

Please contact Vico Publishing for further information.

Book design by Studio 31
www.studio31.com

Printed in the U.S.A.

IN MEMORY

OF ALL WHO PERISHED ON

SEPTEMBER 11, 2001.

ACKNOWLEDGMENTS

To my friend and partner, Tommy, for sharing his original vision with me on that fateful day and collaborating with me to bring his vision to life. I am forever grateful to have had the honor of writing this story. Thank you.

To our families, thank you for your love and unconditional support.

To Bill Corsa for believing in our unusual project and showing us the way.

To Nel Yomtov for his quick and thorough polishing.

To Jim Wasserman for his help with design and production.

To Louie Gasparro for his Fireman cover drawing, and Romik Safarian for his oval of the Brooklyn Bridge and New York City Skyline, as well as the chapter opening illustrations.

To Genarosa Vito and Jeffrey Moses Coleman for watching over us every step of the way. We love you and miss you very much.

CONTENTS

Preface   11

Chapter One: A Little Boy in a Big City   13

Chapter Two: The Firehouse   16

Chapter Three: A Visit to the Twin Towers   20

Chapter Four: Taking the First Step   24

Chapter Five: Competition Day   28

Chapter Six: The Race   31

Chapter Seven: The Dream   35

Chapter Eight: A Race Against Time   38

Chapter Nine: A Hero's Welcome   42

The Morals of Our Story   44

What Can We Learn from Jesus' Story?   47

Fire and Home Safety Checklist   48

Preface

September 11, 2001, dawned on New York City as a picture-perfect morning, with brilliant sunshine and crystal clear blue skies. Summer had unofficially ended, the new school year had begun, and the city streets buzzed with activity.

The steel and glass skin of the World Trade Center in Lower Manhattan boldly reflected the start of the new day. Within minutes, however, the twin monoliths that symbolized economic prosperity and Western ideals of freedom and independence would vanish from the New York skyline. The sun had risen over the Twin Towers for the last time.

Martin E. Coleman and Thomas J. Vito stood side-by-side on the top floor of the Financial District office building where they worked. They were looking out their office windows directly at the World Trade Center towers at the very moment the North Tower was hit by a commercial passenger jet flown by terrorist hijackers. The events that unfolded that day transformed the world and the relationship between the two men, from coworkers to lifelong friends.

The tragedy of 9/11 is a difficult story to explain to anyone, especially children. Yet it must be discussed to honor and remember those who perished and the brave souls who sacrificed their lives for others that day.

Born from the ashes of 9/11 is this story of a young boy's journey toward becoming a man. He lives his life with honor, selflessness, and bravery. He demonstrates that perseverance, determination, and faith in God can help overcome personal challenges and obstacles.

God bless the souls of those who lost their lives or lost their way in the darkness of 9/11. We commemorate them with our story of hope and light.

CHAPTER ONE

A Little Boy in a Big City

Jesus was a little boy who was born and raised in Brooklyn, New York. He lived happily with his younger sister, mother, and father on a quiet, tree-lined street of modest brownstone homes. Many local shops provided the neighborhood goods and services. On his block were a grocer, a shoemaker, a baker, a butcher, a barber, a tailor, and even a pet store with little kittens and puppies playing in the storefront window.

Many of the residents and business owners in the neighborhood knew young Jesus, and they knew him to always wear a warm smile. He loved to say hello to everyone. When he was in the first grade, he and his dad would walk home from school together and stop for a few moments to chat with many of the shop owners. They looked forward to seeing him each afternoon.

Whenever Jesus stopped by the grocery, the owner, Paul, gave him a grandfatherly pat on his head. He tousled Jesus' hair, pinched his cheek, and gave him a shiny red apple or a yellow banana. Jesus would politely say, "thank you," and Paul would tell Jesus to make sure he said hello to his parents for him. "I will," Jesus promised, as he would turn and skip down the sidewalk on his way home.

Jesus particularly looked forward to stopping at the firehouse located next door to his home. Engine Company No. 1 was the center of all activity for the community. The neighborhood block parties, local meetings, and community functions all took place there.

The firehouse had been located in the same two-story, red brick building for more than one hundred years. More important than its appearance were the men and women stationed in the firehouse. They made the firehouse feel comforting and welcoming. Inside the firehouse, a commemorative mural showed a huge bald eagle holding an American flag. The painting proudly honored the brave men and women of Engine Company No. 1 who had sacrificed their lives in the line of duty on September 11, 2001.

Over the years, Jesus got to know everyone in the firehouse by name. The battalion even made him an honorary captain. Jesus loved to help the crew do small chores. He swept the front steps, polished the brass pole, and hosed the trucks after they returned from an alarm. He even gave Sparky, the firehouse Dalmatian, a bath every week.

When Jesus finished his homework and daily chores, he played on the front stoop of his house with his toy airplanes, racing cars, and trucks. He especially enjoyed the hook-and-ladder and pumper fire truck set Santa Claus had given him for being a good boy.

Jesus wrote a letter to Santa at the North Pole every year to remind him that he had been helpful to his parents by always finishing his household chores. He took out the garbage, swept the porch, kept his room tidy, sorted the laundry, and did everything his mother asked him to do. He also told Santa that he helped the firefighters at Engine Company No. 1 and hoped that one day he would become a strong and brave firefighter, too.

One thing Jesus loved more than anything else was pretending to be a New York City firefighter. Dressed in his bright yellow rain slicker and rubber boots, he would drift off into an imaginary world of firefighting where he would race into a burning building to save lives. Jesus always prayed to God that he would have the strength and courage needed to become a firefighter.

Jesus built make-believe neighborhoods with the large cardboard breadboxes and old wooden pallets from the alleyway behind the Italian bakery. He often played "firefighter," pretending to race into a burning building to save a helpless neighbor.

At other times, he imagined he was a first responder to a blaze. He would spray the windows of his neighbor's house with his mother's garden hose. His game would always come to an abrupt halt when his mother noticed water pouring down the side of the house.

Alarmed, she would shout, "Jesus! Turn off that garden hose! You're wasting water! People in many places around the world walk miles every day just to get enough fresh water to survive. Now put away that hose and come in for dinner!"

CHAPTER TWO

THE FIREHOUSE

A shiny, copper placard hung next to the entrance of the firehouse. It honored all the firefighters who had sacrificed their lives to serve and protect the neighborhood. Inscribed on the placard were words from New York City's first European settlers, the Dutch: "*Een Draght Mackt Maght.*" The phrase means, "In Unity, there is strength." The Dutch chose it as the motto for their newly established homeland.

The Dutch settlers from the Netherlands had arrived to find a wilderness of pristine forests, meadows of colorful wildflowers, and lush green wetlands. Slowly meandering streams and flowing brooks teemed with all types and sizes of fish. American Bald eagles and red-tail hawks spread their giant wings as they majestically soared over the forests and ponds that dotted the landscape below. Massive snowy owls guarded the night sky, quietly waiting for a field mouse to stir. Beaver families tirelessly cut down trees to build their dams. Red fox, raccoons, squirrels, deer, and black bears also roamed the forest and hills of this untamed landscape. Eventually, this expanse of wilderness would later be transformed into the bustling and thriving metropolis of New York City.

Between the two garage doors of the firehouse, "Old Glory's" red, white, and blue stars and stripes waved proudly in the gentle breeze. Next to the doors was a window where a firefighter always sat on watch duty. Firefighting vehicles, polished to a sparkling mirrored shine, were parked inside. The garage also housed a red hook-and-ladder firefighting truck emblazoned with a reflective "No. 1" on the doors. A tall, boxy ambulance with ECNALUBMA stamped across its broad hood stood next to the truck.

Charcoal-black firefighter suits with shiny yellow reflector stripes hung inside the firehouse side-by-side in a perfect line. Waiting like soldiers, boots and coveralls stood at the ready. When the fire alarm clanged, the firefighters would spring into a carefully practiced routine ensuring they would get to the emergency quickly and safely.

Ever since he could remember, the sights and sounds coming from the firehouse had always excited Jesus. He would hear the firefighters check their chainsaws and "Jaws of Life" to make sure this equipment was ready to use at a moment's notice. In the business of saving lives, every second counted! He watched the battalion uncoil and recoil the hoses after each emergency to make sure they were not crimped or kinked.

Jesus loved the larger-than-life red trucks and the shiny brass pole the firefighters used to slide down from their second-floor bunkroom when the emergency bell clattered. Most of all, he enjoyed watching the brave and rugged firefighters as they manned their powerful trucks and zoomed away to face unpredictable perils and dangers.

The bright flashing lights, the *"ding, ding, ding"* of the fire bell, the blaring siren, and the *groooowwl* of the powerful diesel engines created a booming concert warning people to get out of the way. But for Jesus, the revving engines sounded like sweet, harmonious music. The blaring sirens and air horn blasts made his eyes light up and sparkle. The hairs on the back of his neck stood at attention. The excitement gave him goose bumps up and down his arms.

It was pure magic and delight. He could think of nothing else he would rather do than watch his heroes set out to save lives. This was truly work for the sake of God.

Whenever he heard the urgent sound of the firehouse alarm, Jesus stopped what he was doing. He ran as quickly as his legs would carry him just to catch a glimpse of the engine charging from the firehouse. As the trucks throttled past him, Jesus snapped to attention and stiffly raised his right hand to salute the brave men and women speeding off to face danger.

Jesus imagined where these firefighters were going and how it might feel to be like them. He felt in his heart that God destined him to become a firefighter when he was grown up, too. God called on Jesus because God knew that Jesus possessed the very special qualities one needs to put oneself in harms' way every day. Firefighting is dangerous work. Heaven could be a split second away for these tireless and brave warriors.

Each night, Jesus turned down his sheet and blanket, knelt beside his bed, and prayed to God. He asked for good health, safety, the well being of his family, and protection of all firefighters and first responders. Jesus also prayed for peace and bounty for all of God's creatures around the world. He thanked God for another wonderful and blessed day.

Then Jesus turned off the bedside lamp and crawled into bed. As he drifted off to sleep, he imagined himself as a strong, brave firefighter.

CHAPTER THREE

A Visit to the Twin Towers

Jesus had learned that every firefighter had to be able to climb tall ladders and tolerate extreme heights. But he felt very uncomfortable in those situations. Often, when he thought about his fears, he recalled the time his parents took him to the observation deck of the Twin Towers to celebrate his fifth birthday.

When they arrived and looked up at the tops of the towers piercing through the high, swirling clouds, Jesus' knees trembled and his legs felt weak. Dizziness swept over him. It was far more grandiose than he ever imagined a building could be. "Wow! Do those buildings go all the way to heaven, Daddy?" he asked.

Once inside, Jesus' stomach sank to his feet as the elevator rapidly ascended up the tower. His eardrums tightened from the change in the air pressure as the elevator climbed higher. When the elevator reached the top, the doors opened to reveal bright rays of sunshine streaming through the floor-to-ceiling windows around the perimeter of the building.

Jesus felt safe in his father's arms as they looked out at Manhattan's gorgeous blue harbor. Tiny sailboats seemed to dance across the ripples in the water. Jesus and his father proudly admired the symbolic flame of the torch held by "Lady Liberty," the 150-foot-tall Statue of Liberty, which stood in the harbor.

They could see the massive stone towers of the Brooklyn Bridge on each side of the East River that separated Manhattan from Brooklyn. Its sweeping high-wire cables appeared to miraculously hover over the swirling waters of the East River below. From the opposite side of the tower they could see the sharply pointed spire of the Empire State Building reaching into the sky.

The moment Jesus peered down at the ant-sized people and the toy-sized cars his stomach felt queasy and his hands trembled. He was overcome by the extreme height. His stomach did dippity-dos and flip-flops, his knees wobbled, and his heart beat as rapidly as a drum. Behind him, other children giggled with excitement as their parents showed them the sites through the windows of the tower.

Jesus closed his eyes and wrapped his arms tightly around his father's legs. His father affectionately stroked the back of his head to comfort him.

"It's okay, Jesus. It's okay. Don't look down again."

"Daddy, can we please leave now? I'm very frightened to be this high in the sky. *Can we go down right now?*"

All little Jesus wanted to do was return to the street where he could feel the firm ground under his feet. Jesus prayed to God that he would quickly and safely return to the comfort of the solid ground below.

"Of course, Jesus. Hold my hand and we'll be down in just a few moments," his father replied.

When they finally reached the ground floor, Jesus let out a deep sigh of relief and thanked the Lord for his safe return to the street level.

"That was really, really scary, Daddy. Next time, can we just go to Central Park and ride the carousel?"

The frightening experience caused Jesus to asked himself, "How can I possibly become a brave firefighter if I'm afraid to ride an elevator high into the sky and look down to the street from a tall building?"

But Jesus was determined to hide his fear. Even though his father told him it was okay to be afraid of heights, Jesus thought his fear was a sign of weakness and unworthiness. After all, many children that day were laughing and enjoying the spectacular views. He wondered why God would allow him to feel so uncomfortable and fearful if it was his destiny to become a firefighter.

"Certainly," he thought, "something must be wrong with me to feel so scared by heights."

Each night before he went to sleep and each Sunday at Mass, Jesus prayed that God would help him overcome the paralyzing fear that took hold of him whenever he had to climb a ladder or a tree.

Despite his prayers, Jesus' fear did not go away. Maybe God wasn't listening to him? Jesus thought perhaps he needed to pray more often. He felt he simply was not reaching God. Meanwhile, he invented excuses so no one would discover his insecurity. Jesus simply did not believe in himself, but he did not understand this.

Jesus enjoyed playing many different sports. He was good at skateboarding, soccer, football, baseball and basketball. Sometimes when Jesus and his friends played in the park, his friends would climb to the top of the giant trees. Jesus either would make excuses or would hang from a branch that he could reach by jumping. While his friends were perched high up in the top branches, Jesus felt left out of the group. He wished with all his heart that he wasn't afraid of heights. Even worse than his fear was being teased by the other kids who saw that he was afraid to join them high in the trees.

When summer arrived, all his friends enjoyed making big splashes at the pool when they jumped from the high-dive platform. But Jesus always found a reason to avoid jumping with them.

"Hurry up, Jesus! It's your turn to jump," his friends cried out. "Are you chicken? *Bock, bock, bock!* they teased as they flapped their arms up and down.

"I'm not scared! I could make a bigger splash than any of you, but I have to go home now. I wish I could stay and hang out. Next time I'll jump first!"

But Jesus knew better, and he thought to himself, "If only that were the truth!"

CHAPTER FOUR

Taking the First Step

Despite his fear of heights, Jesus continued to dream of one day becoming a firefighter. Although it was a challenging goal, he had faith that God would help him find a way to succeed. It was now eleven years since his birthday trip to the top of the World Trade Center. That fateful day had left a mark on his memory, and so he worried that his fear would prevent him from realizing his dream.

One day on his way home from morning Mass, Jesus noticed a small poster hanging on the door of the firehouse. The poster advertised open tryouts for the borough's junior fire corps team, the Brooklyn Blazers. Jesus went inside and asked Mike, the captain on duty, about the team. Captain Mike explained that the Brooklyn Blazers was a competitive team of young city kids who had a passion for adventure and a desire to challenge themselves mentally and physically. Jesus wondered aloud why he had never heard about the team.

"Well, maybe until now you weren't looking to join such a team," Captain Mike said. "Perhaps you're now ready to challenge yourself in ways you never imagined before."

At that moment, a lightbulb seemingly turned on inside

Jesus' head. He thought, "If I join the Brooklyn Blazers, I might be able to overcome my fear of heights. Then I'd no longer have to avoid feeling ashamed of myself like I did when I felt too afraid to climb the trees with my friends."

He thought, too, that perhaps God was sending him a message.

To be admitted to the corps, an applicant had to demonstrate excellence in both citizenship and academic performance. In the corps, junior firefighters learned the value of hard work, self-discipline, teamwork, and, most importantly, confidence. They wore their own special firefighter "turnout" safety gear, which included a fire helmet, a jacket, coveralls, and fireproof boots like those worn by real firefighters.

It was a special honor to be a member of the Brooklyn Blazers. With this honor came a great amount of responsibility and personal sacrifice. A commitment to the team would require Jesus to sacrifice his free time. He would no longer have the luxury of playing with his high school friends after school. He would have to practice with the team and still find time to do his homework and his chores.

Every weekend the Brooklyn Blazers trained with veteran firefighters. The Blazers learned the importance of being physically fit, doing well in school, respecting authority, helping out with chores at home, and contributing to their community. The group engaged in a variety of physical activities, including some that required them to climb ladders and rappel down ropes. Jesus was able to manage these modest heights—and so he was able to keep his secret hidden from everyone.

The initial tryout was designed to test the level of each applicant's physical fitness. Jesus was confident that he was fit because of all of his physical activity and exercise. "This is going to be a cinch," he thought to himself.

And a cinch it was. Jesus ran the one-mile jog without breaking a sweat, and did twenty-five pushups, ten pull-ups, twenty-five sit-ups, and fifty jumping jacks easily. His excellent performance won Jesus an invitation to join The Brooklyn Blazers. He had made the squad! Jesus' parents were thrilled that he made the team, and they happily gave him permission to join. Jesus thanked God for his good performance.

Following his acceptance, Jesus endured months of hard training in preparation for a competition between the other junior fire corps teams throughout the city. They would compete with the Staten Island Surf Riders, the Manhattan Mavericks, the Bronx Blasters, and the Queens Questers. During the training, Jesus made many new friends with the other young men and women.

Jesus loved learning how to coil and uncoil the heavy hoses, how to put on the turnout gear and boots properly, and how to open and close off a fire hydrant. The group jogged together in the park and did stretching exercises and calisthenics. They even learned how to make an old-fashioned spaghetti-and-meatball dinner for the entire firehouse. The Blazers joked that it was easier to coil the spaghetti than to coil the hoses!

Jesus' favorite part of the battalion dinner was saying grace for the meal. He took pride as everyone relaxed and enjoyed the food he had helped prepare. His least favorite job was washing and drying the dishes and then putting them away! Yet, with each task he accomplished, no matter how big or small, he felt more confident and thanked God for this liberating feeling.

Jesus felt he could ace the big competition, but something still troubled him—he was still afraid of heights. What would he do when he had to climb the tall ladder and experience the feelings that haunted him for so many years? He spent many restless nights fearful that his teammates would discover his weakness.

Jesus secretly hoped he would somehow be forced to withdraw from the competition before his fear was revealed. He imagined bowing out of his commitment without admitting his fear. This fantasy gave him a false sense of relief. He desperately wanted this feeling to go away because he had trained too hard to be part of the competition, no matter what the outcome.

Jesus believed he could only pray for a way out.

CHAPTER FIVE

COMPETITION DAY

The day of the competition finally arrived and Jesus now faced his biggest challenge—the New York City Regional Junior Fire & Rescue Corps' Team Obstacle Course and Relay Race. It was a spectacular spring day. The sun shined brightly, and the leaves were budding new life on bare tree branches. Birds happily chirped, and puffy white clouds floated like giant balls of cotton candy in the sky.

Jesus had been selected to run the anchor, or final, position of the relay race for the Brooklyn Blazers. As his team's final runner in the last leg of the race, it was his responsibility to keep the Blazers' lead if they had one, or pass his opponents if his team was behind.

But Jesus faced a major problem: in the final round of the competition, all the participants had to climb up and down a twenty-foot-tall ladder. Jesus had known this moment of truth would come, but he had blocked it out of his mind.

Jesus did not want to disappoint his teammates. They looked up to him because he was always the first to arrive at practice and the last to leave. Although he put in extra effort at every team practice, Jesus always felt that he still could improve his performance. Jesus was a born leader, but he did not see this quality in himself.

Unknowingly, Jesus was trying to compensate for his fear of heights by being the very best in every other aspect of the race. He tried to convince himself that when the time came for him to anchor the race and climb the tall ladder, he would conquer his fear. If only he had told his coach about his fear, the coach would have worked with him to overcome it.

When the final round of the competition arrived, the Brooklyn Blazers were tied with the Queens Questers. The Questers had won the competition for the past five years. They had owned the bragging rights for this coveted trophy for a long time, and everyone in Brooklyn feared that the Blazers might never again display the trophy on their home turf. The people of Brooklyn and Jesus' teammates were counting on him to help win the trophy and bring it home to the neighborhood firehouse.

Jesus and his teammates surveyed the obstacle course, where the two teams would compete side by side. The first part of the race was an all-out sprint to a monkey bar ladder, followed by a tricky rope swing over a shallow moat of water. The moat led to a shaky, narrow balance beam. Once off the beam, each competitor had to roll a heavy rubber tire to the top of a long dirt ramp and dash to the next part of the course.

In the second part of the relay, competitors first had to quickly dress in their firefighter gear. Then they had to climb an eight-foot ladder to the top of a wall and rappell down a safety line on the other side. From there they had to crawl on their bellies through a dark, winding maze of narrow cement pipes. When they emerged from the pipes, they were required to coil a double-jacket fire hose, hoist the coil onto their shoulder, and race fifty yards to a dirt ramp.

Putting down the coiled hose, they would then roll another rubber tire to the top of a second dirt ramp. After the ramp was the twenty-foot ladder! The final relay competitor for each team had to scale the ladder, grab a red flag at the top, and bring the flag down. Back on the ground they would then pick up a Halligan bar, a pick-like tool that firefighters used to break down doors or tear apart door locks. The first team across the finish line with the flag and the Halligan bar was the winner.

During practice Jesus had climbed a short ladder, but nothing had prepared him for a challenge this daunting. He looked at the tall ladder and wished he could ignore his fear. He felt his body stiffen. His mouth went dry, making it hard for him to swallow. Time slowed to a crawl.

Jesus' mind raced. While his eyes measured the fearsome height of the ladder, his knees trembled uncontrollably. A giant bead of sweat raced down his face and plopped onto his firefighter boots. Jesus took two long deep breaths as he struggled to calm his fear.

"We're all counting on you, Jesus!" his teammates shouted. "Bring it home!!"

The coach patted Jesus on the shoulder. "Go get 'em, sport! You can do it!"

TWEEEEET! The referee loudly blew the whistle to signal the start of the race. And they were off!

CHAPTER SIX
THE RACE

The Blazers and the Questers were almost even when Jesus' turn to race came. He started out strong, sprinting down the field as fast as his legs would carry him. He could hear the rush of wind blow past his ears and feel the uneven ground beneath his feet. He jumped up to the monkey bars and raced, hand-over-hand, rung after rung, until he reached the final bar and released his tight grip. Jesus was in the lead!

Jesus dashed ahead, grabbed the rope swing, lifted himself up, and propelled himself over the moat of water. When he cleared it, he released the thick rope and dropped himself to the ground. Then he hopped on the log beam, keeping his balance as he skipped across the bark.

Jesus widened his lead over the racer beside him. Despite his own loud huffing and puffing, Jesus could hear the far-away voices of the crowd cheering, *"Go, Jesus, go!"*

Jesus handled the first tire roll with ease, quickly rolling it up the dirt ramp. He pulled on his firefighter gear and without thinking went up the stepladder over the wall and rappelled down. Quickly down and through the pipes he went. He came out breathing hard, but coiled up the hose, pulled it to his shoulder, and raced to the ramp. It took all his strength

31

to keep going. He reached the ramp and rolled the second tire to the top.

Then, coming off the ramp he turned to face the obstacle he most dreaded . . . the ladder!

Mustering all of his willpower, he grabbed the ladder rails as he took his first step up. His hands were sweaty in his gloves, yet he took several more rungs even more quickly than he thought he could.

Jesus' heavy gear and helmet began to weigh him down. As he neared the halfway point of the ladder, he felt as if he were not moving at all. He glanced upward. The top of the ladder seemed to vanish into the clouds that floated in the sunny sky above. Although he felt faint and a bit dizzy, the rays of sunshine gave Jesus a glimmer of hope. "Maybe I *can* do it," he thought.

But Jesus' hope quickly faded as his fear overtook him, and he froze in place. His mind raced back to his fifth birthday when his father took him to the top of the Twin Towers. In a flash, he felt as if he were back in that moment. Jesus felt helpless.

Sweat poured into his eyes, stinging them and forcing tears of anguish. He pushed on, bravely taking another step. His feet and hands trembled uncontrollably.

"Don't look down," he cautioned himself. "Whatever you do, don't look down!

Then, suddenly, it happened. A few rungs from the top of the ladder, Jesus lost his focus. His nerves had finally got the best of him. Jesus missed a rung and his feet slipped. The weight of his body and his heavy gear overwhelmed his strength. Panicking, he desperately grabbed the rung and dangled in midair. Kicking and flailing, Jesus could feel his fingers slipping from the rung. He kicked faster and faster, frantically trying to find the rung that was just an inch beneath his feet. The crowd below gasped in horror.

Jesus' entire body tightened and ached. His pulse raced wildly, and his chest heaved up and down as he labored to catch his breath. His heart pounded thunderously in his ears. Time seemed to stand still, and the world around him became silent.

"Hold on, Jesus! Don't panic," the crowd shouted to him.

Finally, Jesus could hear his coach's voice break through the silence. "Lower your foot slowly and you'll feel the next rung below!"

As his grip loosened, Jesus felt a slight push as if the wind had blown his foot closer to the ladder rung. He muttered a prayer to God under his breath. In that moment, he made a promise to always be truthful no matter how challenging that might be. His foot reached the rung below. He could feel the steel toe of his fire boot tapping against the metal rung as he slid his foot to the center.

Although he was safe for the moment, Jesus stood frozen with fear, unable to reach the top of the ladder. He could not even look up at the red flag, which was just beyond his reach. He began to make his way back down the ladder. The race was over for Jesus and his teammates.

Once again, the Brooklyn Blazers had lost the epic battle to their rivals, the Queens Questers. Everyone was sad and disappointed, especially Jesus. He believed he had let down his team.

Jesus, head bowed, slowly slumped back toward his coach and teammates. Each of them offered kind words of encouragement.

"It happens to the best of us."

"We'll get 'em next time."

"You tried your hardest, and that's all anyone could ask of you."

Jesus was choked up as he began to speak.

"I'm sorry for letting you down, guys. I didn't have the courage to tell you that since I was young, I've always been afraid of heights. I never thought that my fear would cause us to lose this race. I apologize—and I pray you'll forgive me."

Jesus sat on the bench, rested his weary arms on his knees, and covered his face with his hands. He felt better for telling the truth, but he still felt awful about losing. His teammates rallied around him and told him it was okay. The coach congratulated Jesus for having the courage to face his fear and apologize to his teammates.

Despite their kind words, Jesus was unable to accept the defeat. That night Jesus looked in the mirror and tried to understand why God had challenged him in this way. He asked God to help him understand why this happened. He asked God for guidance. He thought that because he acknowledged his challenges to God, God would have at least permitted him to finish the race.

CHAPTER SEVEN

The Dream

That night Jesus barely touched his favorite meal, Mom's delicious spaghetti and meatballs. He asked his parents if he could be excused from the dining table. His parents gave their permission, thinking that Jesus needed some time by himself to sort through his feelings.

As he climbed the stairs to his bedroom, he heard the fire station bell. *Clang, clang! Clang, clang!* He then heard the garage doors clatter as they rolled up to allow the engines to race to the call.

The firefighters shouted instructions to one another as they jumped into their emergency vehicles. Jesus heard the doors of the trucks slam shut. He could see the emergency lights as they cast a red glow on the walls of his bedroom. The fire engines' blaring sirens sounded a high-pitched warning. The engines roared to life, and the engine company sped off to an emergency somewhere in the borough.

But Jesus was tired from the day's events, and besides, he felt unworthy of seeing the firefighters off to the emergency call. He flopped on his bed and fell fast asleep.

Jesus' parents peeked inside his room and found him sleeping. They turned off the lights, tucked the covers around him, and kissed him on his forehead. They quietly tiptoed out of the room and pulled his bedroom door closed. They knew it would take time for their son to get over his feeling of disappointment.

His parents were most proud of him for serving as a role model and facing his fear. Jesus had given his best effort, and even though Jesus thought he came up short, it is all anyone or God could ask of him.

Ultimately, Jesus' parents knew that he had learned a lot about himself by competing in the race. God had tested Jesus' mental and physical strength, and Jesus learned that his faith in God was strong and unwavering. Most of all, he learned a very valuable lesson: telling the truth is very important.

His parents realized that it would take Jesus time to understand these lessons. They believed that God has a plan for everyone and that it simply was not Jesus' moment to bring home a first place trophy for his team this year.

During the middle of the night, Jesus was awakened briefly by the sounds of the firefighters responding to another call. He drifted back into a deep slumber, dreaming about the obstacle course race he had failed to complete that day.

In his dream, Jesus gracefully rappelled down the zip line and scrambled on his hands and knees through the obstacle course. Effortlessly, he climbed up and down the ladder. As he dreamed of racing toward the finish line, Jesus was awakened by loud, desperate cries for help.

"Fire! Help! God help us!"

Because his dream had been so vividly real, Jesus awoke feeling tired as if he had actually been running. Again, he heard cries coming from outside his bedroom window.

"Help! Please help! Help us! Hurry!!"

Was he still dreaming? Jesus rubbed his eyes, shook his head back and forth, and peered at the alarm clock. It was 3:00 a.m. He threw back his bed covers and raced to the bedroom window.

Across the street, Jesus could see shooting flames and heavy black smoke pouring from the window of an apartment! The fire quickly grew into an intense blaze. Jesus looked to the firehouse next door. The garage doors were still open, and the garage was empty. The trucks had not returned from the earlier emergency call.

Glancing back to the apartment building, he saw a woman leaning out of a window. She was frantically waving her right arm, trying to catch the attention of anyone walking by. In her left arm, she was tightly clutching a bundle of blankets.

Jesus' neighbor was in grave danger—and time was running out.

CHAPTER EIGHT

A RACE AGAINST TIME

Without hesitating, Jesus sprang into action! He pulled out his Brooklyn Blazers equipment bag from under his bed and quickly zipped it open. He jumped into his overalls, put on his fireproof jacket, and pulled on his boots. Grabbing his helmet, he ran out of his bedroom, and dashed down the stairs and out the front door.

Small bits of burning embers fell to the sidewalk below the burning apartment. Smoke poured from all sides of the building. Jesus sprinted down the street and into the firehouse.

With all his strength, Jesus grabbed a long, aluminum extension ladder and hoisted it above his head. A surge of energy coursed through him as he struggled to carry the ladder across the street to the burning building. His body was aching to stop and rest, but his heart told him to keep going.

A shocked group of neighbors had gathered to watch the flames grow more intense. Jesus leaned the heavy ladder against the building. As he climbed, he felt the increasing heat through his fire retardant gloves. The black smoke was thick and heavy. It burned his eyes and lungs. Jesus could hardly see or breathe. Tears streamed down his face as he climbed closer to the woman at the window.

Jesus prayed to God to protect him from the perils of the fire. He also prayed for the courage to face his fear of heights. The stakes were higher than ever: this was not a competition but a race against time that could mean the difference between life and death. He clenched his teeth and kept moving, never once hesitating. He completely focused on rescuing the woman from the flames as he scrambled up one rung of the ladder and then another, and yet another. He passed the five-foot mark of the tall ladder. He would not look down. *Grab, step. Grab, step. Grab, step . . . Keep three points of contact with the ladder at all times,* Jesus reminded himself. He climbed another five feet, and then another five feet.

Jesus passed the second floor of the building and continued his climb to the third. *Grab, step. Grab, step. Grab, step.* The roar of the fire was deafening. The building walls hissed and popped as the fire burned. Flames danced and leapt from the windows of the burning structure. More crackles and hisses sounded as embers ricocheted off his helmet and jacket and fell to the street below. He could hear the shouts for help from the woman above.

"Hurry! Please! Please help!"

The burning heat and the fear Jesus felt told him that he should retreat and save himself. But his heart and soul told him to keep going and not give up. His heart pounded, as he desperately gasped for air in the choking smoke.

Just as he began to give in, he felt a surge of strength and overwhelming confidence wash over him. He was experiencing the almighty power of God lift his inner spirit and move his legs up the ladder! The exhaustion, and fear he had felt just moments before, vanished in the wave of divine energy. Jesus felt at peace, yet very powerful and in control. He felt at one with God on a mission to save his neighbors from the horrors of the blaze.

As Jesus reached the top rung, he heard the reassuring sound of fire engine sirens approaching, getting louder and louder. He looked in the window of the burning apartment and saw that there was a baby in the bundle of blankets the woman was holding!

There was no time to lose. He motioned for the woman to hand the baby to him. Like an experienced first responder, he stretched out his arm and balanced himself on the ladder. Jesus' voice carried through the thick billowing smoke.

"Hand me the child!"

Looking on in awe and admiration, the people below held their breaths and prayed for the safety of the woman, the baby, and the firefighter. The woman passed the child to Jesus. He cradled the bundle and shielded it under his coat. While holding the baby, Jesus took several steps down the ladder. From below the window he shouted to the woman to climb out onto the ladder.

"I can't! I am afraid!" she cried. With flames shooting all around her, Jesus knew it was a "now or never" moment.

"Have faith. I know you can do this!" Jesus balanced himself as the woman grabbed the ladder rail and pulled herself from the smoke-filled window onto the ladder. As flames burst out the window Jesus ordered the woman to remain calm and to follow him down to the ground.

As they descended the ladder, a fire engine screeched to a halt in front of the building. The crowd let out a cheer as Jesus, mother, and child reached the ground. Two firefighters rushed to Jesus with proud, approving looks on their faces. As he handed the child to one of the firefighters, Jesus pointed to the other windows where people were still trapped. The firefighters quickly charged hose lines and raised ladders. Jesus was confident that everyone would be saved.

Jesus knelt down, closed his eyes, and prayed. He thanked God for the strength to overcome his fear when it had mattered most. As he prayed he began to realize what he had accomplished by overcoming his fear. With God's guidance, Jesus had saved lives!

When he opened his eyes, he saw that the crowd across the street was praying, too. As Jesus got to his feet another fire truck arrived. The firefighters sprang into action, and everyone in the burning building was rescued without injury.

CHAPTER NINE
A Hero's Welcome

The next day Jesus was invited to City Hall. He met the chief of the fire department, the borough president of Brooklyn, the mayor, and the woman and child he had rescued.

"You saved my baby and me! God bless you!" she tearfully thanked him.

Jesus told her that he felt blessed to be chosen by God to save them and credited God for making him brave. He thanked God for the opportunity to be prepared and capable to fulfill his moral obligation to help fellow human beings.

The mayor declared Jesus a hero for his selfless act of courage and bravery and named him an honorary member of the city's "Bravest." Jesus received a ceremonial Key to the City. Photographers, newspaper journalists, and television reporters competed to get an interview with this new, real-life hero.

Jesus was humbled to receive such praise, but he did not consider himself a hero. He simply did what he felt he should do and what anyone in the same situation would try to do.

Through all his dreams of becoming a firefighter, Jesus had never imagined he would experience anything like this.

He was just a teenager, yet he had faced a life-or-death challenge and had prevailed. His family, friends, coach, and teammates were all proud of his heroic actions. He had performed to the best of his God-given abilities at the most crucial moment in time. He felt the spirit inside him and embraced the knowledge he had been chosen by God to help save lives.

In the brief statement Jesus made to the press and the public, he refused to take credit for his deeds.

"Last night, the quick response of the firefighters and the power of prayer and faith saved everyone from the deadly grip of a ferocious fire. I am honored and thankful to our Lord and Father for bestowing on me the strength, courage, and preparation needed to face the challenge He set before me. I am now ready for the responsibilities of the role I have dreamed of my whole life. This honor is not for me but rather for the firefighters and first responders who have the courage to face every emergency and selflessly risk their lives with each fire they battle to protect our community. God bless them all."

The Morals of Our Story

Discussion Questions

Book Clubs, literature circles, and classroom reading groups can use these discussion points to encourage children to get the most from this story. Along with new words they may learn in each chapter, the questions below will help children think about the issues faced and decisions made as the story unfolds. Further information can be found at www.vicopublishing.com.

Chapter One: A Little Boy in a Big City

How do you help your parents around the house?

Who or what do you like to pretend to be? Why? What is most fun about this for you?

What do you dream of doing when you grow up?

Chapter Two: The Firehouse

Why is the word *ambulance* spelled backward on the hood of the vehicle?

Have you ever been inside a firehouse? What did you find most interesting inside the firehouse?

What does bravery mean to you?

Chapter Three: A Visit to the Twin Towers

Are you afraid of heights? If so, what scares you about heights?

Did you ever feel sad or frustrated because you could not do something your friends could do?

If you have, what was it that you could not do?

Were you able to overcome this problem? If so, how did you do accomplish this?

Chapter Four: Taking the First Step

What was Jesus' secret?

What kinds of activities do you participate in after school or on the weekend?

What do you enjoy most about these activities?

Have you ever told anyone about your fears? If so, how did this make you feel?

Chapter Five: Competition Day

What fears have you ever had to face?

How did you face them or overcome them?

Have you ever doubted yourself? If so, why?

Have you ever been a member of a team?

Does your teammates' support give you confidence?

Chapter Six: The Race

Did you ever feel like you failed at something even though you tried your best?

Did you ever let down someone who was counting on you? How did that make you feel?

How did you respond to this feeling? What did you do about it?

Have you ever confessed to telling a lie?

Why did you feel you had to tell a lie in the first place?

Chapter Seven: The Dream

Have you ever been faced with an emergency situation?

If so, what was this situation, and how did you respond?

What, if anything, would you do differently today if you were to respond to the same or a similar situation?

Chapter Eight: A Race Against Time

Was it risky for Jesus to try to rescue the woman and her child?

Do you feel Jesus acted appropriately by attempting to rescue the woman and her child? Explain your answer.

If not, why do you feel this way?

Do you turn to God for guidance?

How does this make you feel?

Do you feel asking God for guidance is helpful to you? If yes, why do you feel this way?

Have you ever accomplished something you thought you were not capable of doing?

How did this make you feel?

What Can We Learn from Jesus' Story?

We encourage you to think about the morals and lessons you can learn from this story. Here are a few you might have discovered while reading about Jesus' experience as a firefighter:

- Honor God in everything you do.
- Give thanks to God for your health and spiritual guidance.
- Be thankful to God for each and every day of your life.
- Faith is a source of strength.
- Love yourself.
- Love your parents.
- Honor your parents.
- Love your family.
- Love your neighbor.
- Be prepared.
- You can overcome your fears.
- No matter what adversity you might face, never give up on your dreams.
- Follow your true passion in life.
- Remain focused on your goals—you can achieve them.
- Always give your best effort in everything you do.
- Strive to be the best person you can be every day.
- Be humble.

FIRE AND HOME SAFETY
INSPECTION CHECKLIST

We pray you never have to face a fire emergency in your home. We encourage you, however, to discuss fire safety with your family and household members to create your own personalized fire safety plan. The following fire safety and prevention tips have been compiled by Michael Gilroy, retired Executive Director and Superintendent of Fire Programs for Nassau County Fire Service Academy in Uniondale, New York. You can learn more about fire safety from the resources listed at the end of this checklist and by visiting your local firehouse.

Understand what fire is:

Fire is a very quick chemical reaction between oxygen and a combustible material or agent resulting in the release of heat, light, flames, and smoke.

For fire to exist, it requires ample levels of oxygen to sustain combustion, sufficient levels of heat to raise the material to ignition temperature, a source of fuel or a combustible agent, and the reaction itself of fire.

Make a home safety plan:

Map out a home fire escape plan and route, periodically practice it with your children, and designate a meeting place safely outside and away from your home.

Plan and practice two escape routes out of the house and each room.

Your local fire department will be happy to come to your home and workplace to inspect your premises for hazards and dangers as well as designate proper locations for devices such as smoke alarms and fire extinguishers.

They will also help you map out an emergency plan and escape route to provide you and your family with a strategy to reach safety in the event of an emergency.

If windows are used as emergency exits in your home, practice using them in the event a fire should break out.

Be sure that all the windows open quickly, freely, and easily.

Home escape ladders are recommended. Store these ladders in a place everyone is familiar with and can access in a moment's notice.

Practice the use of home safety ladders regularly.

Make sure the ladders are not tangles or frayed, and are in excellent working order.

Make a safety plan for your pet:

Be sure to include your beloved pets in your emergency plan, as sadly, they are often helpless victims in a home fire emergency.

Place a Pet Rescue Fire Sticker in windows around your home. (These are free in most pet stores and available through the ASPCA or your local humane society.)

Keep dry brush and combustible agents away from your pets' outdoor home.

Have an emergency kit ready for your pet, including any medicine your pet may need as well as a photo of your pet, food, veterinary paperwork, proof of ownership, and proper vaccinations.

Evacuate your pet with a leash or a pet carrier.

During a fire in the home a pet likely will be terrified and will retreat to a place in the house where he/she feels safe such as under a bed or behind a curtain.

Create an open access in a door leading to the outside just large enough for your pet to escape in the event of heat, smoke and/or fire.

Once you and your family escape the danger of the fire in your home and have arrived at your designated meeting place, call your pet's name to alert him/her of your whereabouts. With luck, your pet will respond to your call.

Show and tell:

Stay low! Show and practice how to crawl low on the floor below the line of smoke, get out of the house, and stay out and away from the danger.

Demonstrate and practice with children how to stop, drop to the ground, and roll if their clothes catch on fire.

Take children to the local firehouse to meet firefighters and see them in their uniforms so they will learn not be afraid of them in case of an emergency.

Make time throughout the year to regularly revisit and practice these important skills. The more you practice, the better prepared your family will be in the event of a fire emergency.

Schedule in your family's calendar the specific dates and times to do your safety reviews, meetings, and escape plan practices. Be sure to reschedule all missed dates and truly commit to making such plans a part of your family's mandatory routine.

Teach your children when, why and how to call 9-1-1 in the event of an emergency, fire, or disaster.

Teach your children when it is *not* appropriate to call an emergency operator dispatcher, and unnecessarily tie up the lines out of fear.

Over 240 million 9-1-1 calls are made each year in the United States. One-third of these are made from wireless phones.

As of January 2012 the United States has 6,131 primary and secondary PSAPs "Public Safety Answering Point" and 3,135 Counties which include parishes, independent cities, boroughs, and census areas.

Teach your children to memorize your home address and phone number and how to conduct themselves on a call with an emergency operator. Practice this phone skill in regularly practice drills.

Test your smoke detectors:

Be sure to familiarize children with the special sound of your smoke detector.

Always check the smoke, radon, and carbon monoxide detectors every month to ensure that they are functioning properly.

Push the detector's button and be certain it gives off a loud noise.

Replace the batteries every six months or no less than once a year with fresh unexpired high-quality batteries.

Install alarms out of the direct path of steam from faucets and showers, and away from path of cooking vapors to avoid frequent false alarms.

Due to the fact that smoke rises, ceiling-mounted smoke detectors should be installed four to twelve inches from the nearest wall.

Wall-mounted detectors should be installed about one foot from the ceiling.

The Home Safety Council[1] recommends that interconnected safety alarms be used in the home because they use a wireless connection and are hardwired with a battery backup, which enable the alarms to act as a uniform network that will work in concert with one another in the event of being triggered.

The Home Safety Council recommends installing monitoring devices in all bedrooms and areas where your family members may nap or sleep.

Monitoring devices should be properly placed at all levels of your home, including your basement, attic, and garage.

---

1   The Home Safety Council® (HSC) is the only national nonprofit organization solely dedicated to preventing home related injuries that result in nearly 20,000 deaths and 21 million medical visits on average each year. Through national programs, partnerships and the support of volunteers, HSC educates people of all ages to be safer in and around their homes. The Home Safety Council is a 501(c)(3) charitable organization located in Washington, DC.

Do not install detectors near windows, ducts, or doors where drafts may interfere with the optimal operation of the device.

The best systems to install are ionization- and photoelectric-type detectors.

Be sure to install the most modern approved safety devices available on the market for smoke, radon, and carbon monoxide detection.

Do not use an alarm more than ten years old.

Use a hearing-impaired strobe alarm that meets requirements set forth by the Americans with Disabilities Act for any family members who are hearing challenged or deaf.

Use escape light alarms where natural light or spillover light is unavailable.

Set house rules:

Keep matches and lighters in a secure location.

Instruct your children to surrender matches and lighters when they find them.

If you must use a kerosene heater, make sure it is in proper working condition.

Inspect exhaust parts of your kerosene heater for carbon buildup.

Be sure the heater has an emergency shut off in case the heater is tipped over.

Always keep kerosene or other flammable liquids stored in approved metal containers and in a well-ventilated storage area outside of the house.

Keep young children away from space heaters, especially when they are wearing nightgowns or other loose clothing that can easily ignite.

Never cover a lamp, and keep a safe distance from fireplaces and wood stoves.

Children should never cook while alone.

In case of fire in your home:

Always sleep with bedroom doors closed. This prevents smoke, gas, and heat from entering the room.

Always feel doors for heat before opening them. If the door is hot, do not open it. Find another route of escape.

Teach children to never hide in closets, under beds, in bathtubs, or in other areas of the home, no matter what the circumstances. Hiding from firefighters hinders their ability to effectively make a successful rescue.

If there is a fire hydrant near your home, you can assist the fire department by keeping the hydrant clear of snow or debris so that in the event it is needed, it can be immediately located.

Keep up-to-date and accurate home and personal inventory files secured in a safe place.

Keep irreplaceable valuables, jewelry, personal family heirlooms and keepsakes, files, and personal firearms in a highly secure water- and fireproof safe or gun safe. Keep an inventory list of your family valuables for reference.

Attempting to extinguish a home fire:

It is recommended to have at least one fire extinguisher on each level of your home.

However, despite having fire extinguishers strategically stationed in key locations throughout your home, it is important to note: *The U.S. Fire Administration does not recommend the use of fire extinguishers by untrained persons.*[1] *While this is only a recommendation and may be unrealistic sometimes, it is often easy enough to get training from your local fire department, so make the most of this opportunity to become "trained."*

After getting proper training from your local fire officials, familiarize your family with the types of fire extinguishers and the fire extinguishers that are best suited for your home needs, including but not limited to: water, dry chemical (foam powder filled and pressurized with nitrogen) and carbon dioxide made for different classes of fires.

The basic steps of using a fire extinguisher include: PASS—**P**ull the pin, **A**im at the base of the fire not the flames, **S**queeze the lever slowly, and **S**weep from side to side. Always operate an extinguisher from a safe distance at least several feet away, and move closer only as the fire begins to diminish. Each type of extinguisher recommends a proper distance for operation and discharge.

Fire extinguishers are designed to smother a fire and prevent further combustibility. For example, *never* use a water extinguisher on a grease, electrical, or Class D (combustible metals like magnesium or titanium) fire as the flames will spread and make the fire bigger. Water extinguishers are filled with water and pressurized with air. Water is a conductive agent for electricity, and spraying an electrical fire with water can result in a deadly electrocution.

Using the wrong type of extinguisher on a specific kind of fire can quickly make matters worse and be life threatening. Learn the rules of use before equipping your home.

There are many types of extinguishers, therefore base your selection of home extinguishers on the classification needed and the items and areas you wish to protect.

Multi-purpose Dry Chemical (Class A, B, C fires) and Regular Dry Chemical (usual agent is sodium bicarbonate) (Class B, C fires) extinguishers are most commonly used in residential circumstances. Regular Dry Chemical extinguishers are easiest to clean up, needing only vacuuming, sweeping, or flushing with water. They are also nontoxic, noncorrosive, and nonconductive.

Keep them in plain line of site and no more than five (5) feet above the floor.

Do not put them in closets or out of reach as valuable time is lost retrieving an extinguisher placed in an inconvenient location.

Even though a fire extinguisher may not match your décor, do not hide it behind drapes or obstruct it from view. It is not meant to be a decorative piece. It is present in the event a fire breaks out in your home.

The kitchen, workshop, and garage are the best locations for fire extinguishers.

According to U.S. Fire Administration statistics, the kitchen is the location where most home fires break out.

If you have a fire extinguisher in the kitchen, most grease fires can be contained with a proper fire extinguisher. The best location is next to the door of the kitchen entrance.

Do not store the fire extinguisher on or next to the stovetop. In the event of a stove fire, you will likely be able to grab the extinguisher to use it without risking getting burned.

Garages are excellent locations for fire extinguishers because leftover paints, solvents, and building materials are often inappropriately stored here. Store the fire extinguisher by the door.

A typical fire extinguisher has ten (10) seconds of extinguishing power. Be sure to refill a fire extinguisher after each use regardless of the amount used.

Inspect fire extinguishers for visible obstruction or damage in the form of dents, leaks, rust, or visible issues with the pin or pressure gauge. Do so monthly and have the unit professionally maintained and hydrostatically tested once annually to assure proper functionality if and when needed.

Read the extinguisher's instructions carefully before using and consult your local fire department for proper training in its use. Be sure to revisit your training regularly to be adequately prepared for an emergency situation necessitating its use.

We encourage you and your family to spend quality time together learning about fire safety and prevention using the resources provided in this book. It is an opportunity to spend time together for a good cause. There is a lot of useful information available to you on the Internet via credible Web sites and at your local community fire station. Furthermore, we strongly suggest that you consult your local fire safety professionals at your neighborhood fire station to answer any questions you may have and to schedule a visit to your home to evaluate the condition and placement of your safety detectors including radon, smoke, and carbon monoxide.

Your local fire department will gladly come to your home to check the placement and working order of your home extinguishers and detection devices as well as review an exit strategy and plan in the event you and your family find yourselves in an emergency situation. Please take this upon yourself for the safety, security, and well-being of your family and your neighbors' families. Your knowledge, understanding, and preparation are your family's first and sometimes *only* lines of defense against a highly preventable event such as a home fire.

The entire fire community thanks you and commends you for taking the measures necessary to protect your home, property, and most importantly, the health, welfare, and safety of your family.

Valuable online resources
for additional fire safety information:

"Do You Have A Fire Evacuation Plan For Your Pets?" *Dogster for the Love of Dog Blog*. Web. 14 Jan. 2012. http://dogblog.dogster.com/2008/07/28/do-you-have-a-fire-evacuation-plan-for-your-pets/.

"Evacuation Plans and Procedures ETool – OSHA Requirements." *Occupational Safety and*

Fire Extinguisher: 101. Web. 14 Jan. 2012. http://www.fire-extinguisher101.com/.

"FEMA: National Fire Prevention Week 2011." *FEMA / Federal Emergency Management Agency*. Web. 19 Dec. 2011. http://www.fema.gov/news/newsrelease.fema?id=58557.

"Fire Prevention & Safety Checklist." *American Red Cross in Greater New York*. Web. 19 Dec. 2011. http://www.nyredcross.org/?nd=fire_safety_guide.

"Fires | Ready.gov." *Home / Ready.gov*. Web. 19 Dec. 2011. http://www.ready.gov/fires.

"Evacuation Plans and Procedures ETool – OSHA Requirements." *Occupational Safety and*

Health Administration – Home. Web. 14 Jan. 2012. http://www.osha.gov/SLTC/etools/evacuation/portable_required.html.

"Home Safety Council – The Leading Source for Home Safety Tips, Checklists, and Information about Home Fire Safety, Falls Prevention, Poison Prevention, Water Safety, Child Safety, Disaster Preparedness as Well as Many Other Home Safety Topics." *HSC Site Director*. Web. 19 Dec. 2011. http://www.homesafetycouncil.org/index.asp.

Home Safety Products from First Alert, Smoke Alarms, Carbon Monoxide Alarms, Fire Extinguishing Spray, Fire Spray, Home Safety Tests, First Alert. Web. 14 Jan. 2012. http://www.firstalertstore.com.

National Association of Fire Equipment Distributors (NAFED) / Welcome. Web. 14 Jan. 2012. http://www.nafed.org/pubs/fire-watch.cfm.

"News & Publications : Journal® : November/December 2011 : Features." *NFPA*. Web. 19 Dec. 2011. http://www.nfpa.org/public-JournalDetail.asp?categoryID=2318.

"Plan to Protect Yourself & Your Family | Ready.gov." *Home / Ready.gov*. Web. 19 Dec. 2011. http://www.ready.gov/emergency-planning-checklists.

"Safety Information : Fire Prevention Week : About Fire Prevention Week." *NFPA*. Web. 19 Dec. 2011. http://www.nfpa.org/itemDetail.asp?categoryID=1439.

"Safety Information : Fire Prevention Week : For Kids and Families." *NFPA*. Web. 14 Jan. 2012. <http://www.nfpa.org/categoryList.asp?categoryID=2019>.

"Safety Information : For Consumers : Arson & Juvenile Fire Setting : Children Playing with Fire." *NFPA*. Web. 19 Dec. 2011. http://www.nfpa.org/categoryList.asp?categoryID=281.

"Safety Information : For Consumers : Causes : Electrical : Keep Your Community Safe and Energized." *NFPA*. Web. 19 Dec. 2011. http://www.nfpa.org/itemDetail.asp?categoryID=1582.

"UL | Smoke Alarms." Redirecting Page to Browser Language Detected URL. Web. 14 Jan. 2012. http://ul.com/global/eng/pages/corporate/newsroom/storyideas/smokealarms/.

"911 for Kids – 911 Training and Education, 911 Public Education, National 911 Education Month – About 9-1-1 Heroes Awards." *911 for Kids - 911 Training and Education, 911 Public Education, National 911 Education Month – Home*. Web. 14 Jan. 2012. http://www.911forkids.com/content/view/61/1/.

"9-1-1 Statistics." *National Emergency Number Association*. Web. 14 Jan. 2012. http://www.nena.org/?page=911Statistics.

"Safety Information : For Consumers : Arson & Juvenile Fire Setting : Children Playing with Fire." *NFPA*. Web. 19 Dec. 2011. http://www.nfpa.org/categoryList.asp?categoryID=281.

"Safety Information : For Consumers : Causes : Electrical : Keep Your Community Safe and Energized." *NFPA*. Web. 19 Dec. 2011. http://www.nfpa.org/itemDetail.asp?categoryID=1582.

"Fires | Ready.gov." *Home | Ready.gov*. Web. 19 Dec. 2011. http://www.ready.gov/fires.

"Plan to Protect Yourself & Your Family | Ready.gov." *Home | Ready.gov*. Web. 19 Dec. 2011. http://www.ready.gov/emergency-planning-checklists.

"FEMA: National Fire Prevention Week 2011." *FEMA | Federal Emergency Management Agency*. Web. 19 Dec. 2011. http://www.fema.gov/news/newsrelease.fema?id=58557.

"Safety Information : Fire Prevention Week : About Fire Prevention Week." *NFPA*. Web. 19 Dec. 2011. http://www.nfpa.org/itemDetail.asp?categoryID=1439.

The publisher will donate a portion
of the proceeds from the sale of this book to:

Click4Good.org / Near and Dear
The FealGood Foundation
The New York Firefighters Burn Center Foundation

**God bless you,
your family, your community
and the U.S.A.**

ALSO IN THIS SERIES:

What If Jesus Were an American Soldier?
(Hardcover • ISBN: 978-0-9850541-3-7)

What If Jesus Were a Police Officer?
(Hardcover • ISBN: 978-0-9850541-5-1)

VICO
Publishing Inc.

1112 DEVONSHIRE ROAD
HAUPPAUGE, NEW YORK 11788
WWW.VICOPUBLISHING.COM